WHALE WATCH

ALSO BY ADA AND FRANK GRAHAM

Bug Hunters

AN AUDUBON READER

WHALE WATCH

ADA AND FRANK GRAHAM
ILLUSTRATIONS BY D. D. TYLER

DELACORTE PRESS/NEW YORK

Published by
Delacorte Press
1 Dag Hammarskjold Plaza
New York, N.Y. 10017

Designed by Leo McRee

Manufactured in the United States of America

First printing

Library of Congress Cataloging in Publication Data

Graham, Ada.
    Whale watch.

    (An Audubon reader)
    Bibliography: p.
    Includes index.
    SUMMARY: Discusses the whale, the industry
which has slaughtered it almost out of existence,
and efforts to sustain its survival in today's
world.
       1. Whales—Juvenile literature. 2. Whaling—
Juvenile literature. [1. Whales. 2. Whaling]
I. Graham, Frank, 1925–   joint author.
II. Tyler, D. D. III. Title.
QL737.C4G62   599'.5   77-20532

ISBN 0-440-09505-0
ISBN 0-440-09506-9 lib. bdg.

To the memory of Marie Rodell,
conservationist and helpful friend
to so many of us who write about the natural world,
this book is dedicated.

CONTENTS

1
WHALE WATCH

Fog hung over the small rocky island and the sea around it twenty-two miles off the coast of Maine. The water was calm, as if stilled by the very weight of the dense fog. The only sound was the piercing blare of the foghorn coming from the lighthouse that stood on this lonely rock. A tall young man named Ben walked slowly along the narrow platform that circled the lighthouse tower, forty feet above the sea.

Binoculars, which Ben kept with him most of the time, were of no use today, and he had tucked them inside his heavy jacket. He could peer into the fog for only a few feet, but he listened intently for whatever might be out there. The gray sea washed gently against the rocky shore. The foghorn roared again and then there was complete silence.

Whale Watch

"Listen to that," Ben whispered.

Two friends who had come to visit him on the island that day stepped onto the platform beside him. They had also heard the sound as they stood inside the tower, out of the foggy chill. The sound was a loud snort that came from somewhere in the fog near the island. A moment later they heard it again. For several minutes the sounds came at rhythmic intervals, then they grew fainter, and finally faded away.

"Those were fin whales blowing," Ben said to his friends.

He leaned against the tower's great stone blocks for shelter and began to make notes on a printed form. He noted the hour, the temperature, and the time between the sounds they had just heard. Then he put the form into an envelope with a dozen others he had already filled out.

"I think it was a big one, maybe fifty or sixty feet long, because of the time it took to blow," he said. "The big ones take longer to clear their lungs."

Ben, a biology student, has always liked animals of all kinds, but a year or two ago he read a book about whales that changed his life. He became so interested in these

Whale watchers on the lighthouse at Mount Desert Rock.

huge animals and their swift decline toward the edge of extinction that he joined a project called "Allied Whale" at the College of the Atlantic in Bar Harbor, Maine. In the summer he takes turns with other students living for two weeks at a time on this lonely island. The island is Mount Desert Rock, where the U.S. Coast Guard keeps a lighthouse to warn ships away from the rocks. It is seven acres of treeless rock, swept by winds and waves. No plants grow there except hardy grasses and seaweeds.

While Ben lives with the Coast Guardsmen on the island, he is on a constant "whale watch," and he has become an expert in identifying the different kinds of whales by sight and sound. The island stands at a point in the sea where whales pass as they swim up and down the coast during the summer. Like the other students, Ben keeps a record of their numbers, habits, and migrations.

"You wouldn't believe it today, but when the weather is clear you can see the mainland from here," he told his friends.

They were interested in whales too, and had come to the island for the day just before the fog closed in. Ben told them about his life on the island, where he was trying to add to man's small knowledge about these animals.

He was up at dawn every morning. He dressed, then ate a hasty breakfast with the Coast Guardsmen. Dressing even in the middle of summer on this island is not so simple as it sounds, when you are going to spend most of the day standing on a tower above the changeable northern sea. On the warmest day of the summer the temperature climbed only to 72° Fahrenheit (22° Celsius). Ben wore two sweaters, and sometimes a winter coat or a rain slicker over them.

"The cold and dampness can really get to you," he said.

But it is good to be whale watching at Mount Desert Rock in bad weather, because the whales are most active in storms. Ben watched them appear near the island, breaking water at the crest of a wave. A whale would be lifted on a foaming swell of water and then drop suddenly from view. It would seem to fight the raging sea. It found it hard to breathe in the waves that exploded in white fury around it as it came to the surface. Through his binoculars Ben would see the whale's blowholes, or nostrils, begin to open, then a wave would crash over the big animal's back and it would go down for a moment, and rise to blow again.

But Ben had good views of the whales on calm days too. He loved to watch the fin whales—monsters nearly seventy feet long—as they fed around the island, sometimes swimming near the surface and chasing tiny fish. Seabirds flew low over the water, following the whales. When the tip of a whale's mouth caused ripples on the surface, the seabirds flew in front of it to snatch the fish it had stirred up.

A whale can often be told from others of its kind by the shape of its fin or by a scar on its back.

"A few years ago there was a big whale that stayed near the coast of New Hampshire," Ben said. "All the fishermen and scientists could identify this whale even at a long distance because it had a deep V-notch in its back just in front of its fin. The notch was about a foot and a half deep. Maybe a boat ran over it once and hit it with its propeller. Everybody called the whale George."

One day Ben was sitting on the rocks when a fin whale came close to the island. As the whale turned, it rolled over on the surface of the water and Ben could see that its belly was a soft pink. As he had forgotten his camera, he quickly drew a sketch of the whale's fin so that he would be able to recognize it again even if he did not see its belly.

"When you first start looking at whales you usually think they are all black," he said. "That's because of the glaring light reflected by the water all around. But when you have a good pair of binoculars, or you take a good color picture, you can see that whales are many colors— gray or blue, even reddish or orange. I saw one here that was a sort of burnt orange color."

People who watch animals usually have a favorite, and

Ben had one too. It was a young humpback whale, about thirty feet long. The wide finlike tips of a whale's tail are called flukes. This whale had white patches on the underside of its flukes that made it easy to identify.

"The whale stayed around here for about five weeks," Ben said. "We called him Hugh. I guess anything that's very big and homely we think of as a *him*. Anyway, he'd come in very close to the island, and we'd take an iron pipe and bang it on the rocks so it would make a loud ringing sound. The sound would catch Hugh's attention. He would be swimming in a straight line past the shore, but when he heard us banging the pipe he would turn sharply and swim straight toward the island."

Ben heard a whale blowing very close to the island one dark night. He asked the Coast Guardsmen to turn on the searchlight, and in the light they saw Hugh, the humpback whale, swimming in the little cove where visitors to the island sometimes anchored their boats. The water is very shallow in the cove and Hugh's heavy body was nearly touching bottom. In the glare of the light Ben could see the humpback's long white flippers and the knob-like swellings that studded his head like big iron bolts and that help to identify this species.

"We figured he must have been chasing something when he swam into the cove," Ben said. "When morning came Hugh was gone from the cove but there were squid

—little fish that are relatives of the octopus—all over the rocks. They had been trying to get away from Hugh, but we don't know for sure he was after squid."

Ben was delighted to have a humpback whale around the island. These whales had once been common off America's coastline. They are acrobatic animals that spend much time on the surface, leaping from the waves, rolling over, and slapping the water with mighty strokes of their long flippers. These flippers, which are sometimes nearly one-third as long as the whale itself, help observers to tell the humpbacks from all other kinds of whales. The flippers have curious knobs and bumps just like those on its head.

But humpbacks are easy to kill. They often swim close to shore when they migrate, and hundreds of thousands of them have been taken in the last two hundred years by whalers. By the time they were protected through an agreement among the whale-killing nations in 1966, their numbers had dropped to a dangerously low point. They are beginning to recover a little now in the North Atlantic.

"Whales usually keep moving in search of food," Ben

A humpback whale breaching. Each bump on the long flippers corresponds to a joint in its "fingers."

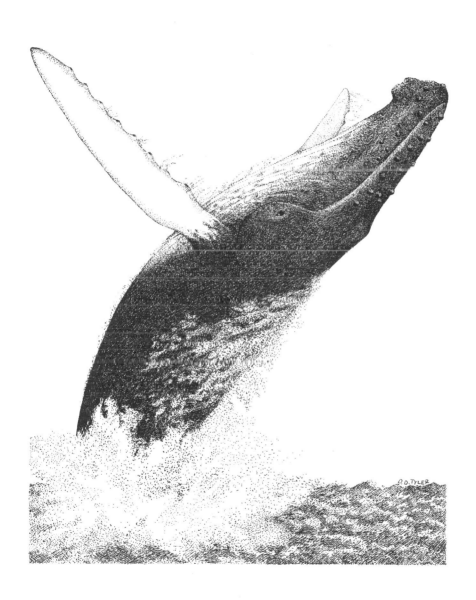

told his friends. "Whatever Hugh was eating must have been staying around here, and that's why Hugh stayed too."

One day Ben put on a wet suit and went for a swim in the cold water around the island. Suddenly he noticed an enormous form rising to the surface nearby; then he saw the knobby head and long white flippers of Hugh.

"It was the greatest thrill of my life to be swimming along beside this great animal," Ben said, his eyes brightening at the memory. "He was only about eight feet away. Then he dove underneath me. I thought he was just playing with me, but I was a little shook up later on when I found out that's the way humpbacks behave when they want to threaten you!"

Not many people have had the experience of swimming alongside a healthy young whale in the open ocean. Just wanting to be in a whale's company, for its own sake, is a new feeling for humanity. A few years ago those feelings were completely different.

2
VOYAGE BETWEEN TWO WORLDS

"No being can reveal more marvelous grace than a whale. Do not think of them as shapeless as I once did. Envision, rather, this magnificent blue whale, as shapely as a mackerel, spending his last ounce of strength and life in a hopeless contest against cool, unmoved, insensate man. Sheer beauty, symmetry, utter perfection of form and movement, were more impressive than even the whale's incomparable size."

These words were written in the year 1912 by another young scientist. His name was Robert Cushman Murphy and he became one of America's most famous students of seabirds. But in that year, before World War I, he was just beginning his career. He set out on a voyage that allowed him to see two worlds—the end of the era of adventurous New England whalers and the frightening new era of mechanized slaughter.

Whale Watch

In 1912, Bob Murphy—tall, athletic, and good-looking
—was a collector of birds for the American Museum of
Natural History in New York City. Collecting birds,
which meant shooting them and preparing their skins for
study by scientists, was an important job in those days.
Museums were trying to make scientific collections of all
the birds in the world. Murphy, who had grown up on
Long Island Sound, knew a lot about boats and the sea.
His special interest was seabirds.

The museum's staff was eager to increase their collection of seabirds from the Southern Hemisphere. They
asked Murphy to go to the South Atlantic Ocean to collect
birds. Few boats sailed to islands near the Antarctic in
those days.

The museum arranged for Murphy to go to the islands
of the South Atlantic on a whaling ship. It was a difficult
job for him. He had just married Grace Emaline Bar-
stow, and the voyage would take him away from his bride
for nearly a year. There were no radios, telephones, or
mail services where he was going.

But Grace encouraged him to go. To let her know just
what the voyage was like, he wrote down the events of
the day every evening, just as a ship's captain does in a
logbook. Murphy called his journal *Logbook for Grace*.
While it gives an account of a young scientist's work at
sea, it also draws a vivid picture of a period of important
change in the whaling industry.

Voyage Between Two Worlds

Bob Murphy sailed for the South Atlantic on the *Daisy*, one of the last of the old sailing ships. It was 123 feet long and had been built in 1872 of oak and chestnut wood, with a deck of yellow pine. The captain was a whaling man from Massachusetts.

Murphy soon learned that he was not on a holiday cruise. Everyone's living space was small and cramped. The water was sour, the food was poor. The diet of canned or dried food was dull, varied only by the fresh fish the crew was able to catch along the way. Murphy lived just as the whaling crews had a hundred years before.

An old whaling ship was like a battleship in many ways. It needed a larger crew than an ordinary ship of its size. For much of the time those extra men had nothing to do. They simply got bored or complained about the food or fought among themselves. But all of them were needed when the ship went into battle against a great whale.

The *Daisy* sailed south into tropical waters. Murphy had brought along a little rowboat called a dory. When the wind died and the sailing ship stopped moving, he sometimes lowered the dory into the water and rowed off to collect birds and sea animals. He shot seabirds called petrels and shearwaters. He caught sharks and other fish and dissected them for study. He dipped his net into the dense masses of seaweed that drifted on the surface of the Sargasso Sea.

"There were fifteen or more kinds of tiny animals living in the floating orange forest," he wrote in his journal, "of which one was a sea-slug, one a worm, one a hydroid, one a fish, and four or more crustaceans. Of the latter, two were little crabs and two long-whiskered prawns. You don't see them until you poke around, because they all look like part of the vegetation."

But for days at a time the crew of the *Daisy* didn't see another living thing. The ship rocked endlessly under the center of the blue dome of sky. They seemed to be imprisoned within the circle of an unbroken horizon. Sometimes Murphy climbed to the top of the mainmast to look around him.

"The distance was ten times as far looking down as up," he wrote. "The motion was extremely disconcerting, particularly the snap at the end of each roll, by means of which the vessel tried to catapult me off into the sea. The deck looked small and queer and usually far off to one side."

Lookouts, called "the eyes of the ship," were stationed at the top of the mainmast to give the signal if a whale came into sight. Sometimes a fin whale was sighted, but no one paid any attention to it. Fin whales—nearly seventy feet long—are able to swim at twelve or fourteen nautical miles an hour, and were much too fast for the small, slow-moving *Daisy* to catch.

But there were moments of high adventure. Murphy had read that when a lookout on a whaling ship sighted a whale he cried, "Thar she blows!" That meant he had seen the spout shot by a whale from its blowholes, when it came to the surface to breathe. But Murphy learned that when the lookouts on the *Daisy* saw one of the kinds of whales for which they were looking, "they go plumb crazy and sing at the top of their lungs."

Murphy was startled by such a cry one morning.

" 'Blo-o-o-o-o-o-o-o-ws,' cried a lookout from his perch on the mast. 'Blo-o-o-o-o-o-o-o-ws. White water! Ah, blo-o-o-o-o-o-o-o-ws!' shouted all four lookouts at once. Even the men on deck sent up the same cry. They ran around in all directions, pulling on their slickers and snatching up pieces of equipment.

"The whole crew sounded and acted like a chorus gone mad," Murphy wrote.

The lookouts had sighted a school of sperm whales, blowing and splashing on the water's surface. The men could tell they were sperm whales because of their lazy, forward-slanting spouts. Sperm whales were highly prized by the New England whalers for the large quantity of oil they contained.

The crew lowered the *Daisy*'s four whaleboats into the water. These light but sturdy boats, thirty feet long and built of white cedar, carried both oars and sails. Six men leaped into each whaleboat and set off after the whales. Bob Murphy was in one of the boats.

A stiff wind whipped the sea into choppy waves. As the boats raised their sails, they were overtaken by a rain squall, and the men were drenched. Crouched in the bow of each boat was the harpooner—the man who would thrust the iron harpoon into the whale. The harpoon line, a stout rope twelve hundred feet long, lay coiled in wooden tubs in the bottom of the boat.

Suddenly Murphy saw a large bull whale come to the surface directly in front of the whaleboat. It was fifty feet long. The harpooner did not throw his harpoon at the whale, but always waited until the small boat was rowed by the crew right up onto the huge mammal's back.

Emiliano, the harpooner in Murphy's boat, knew his job well. Just as the gray back of the whale glided under the boat's sharp prow, Emiliano plunged the heavy harpoon into its right side. The whale leaped forward and upward. Its great blunt head shot out of the water. The powerful flukes slapped against the bottom of the boat as it rushed away, the line rapidly uncoiling behind it.

The little boat was now off on what the older whalemen

Early whaling scene. In front of the whaleboat, a sperm whale is sounding; in the background, one is blowing.

—who sailed out of Nantucket—called a "Nantucket sleigh ride." The crew hastily pulled down the sails and hung on grimly as the whale towed them across the ocean. Finally the whale stopped and rested on the surface. The crew, including Murphy, began to row toward it. Through the rain and choppy sea they approached the whale, the harpoon still sticking from its glistening back.

The men rowed up to the whale. One of the whalers picked up a long, razor-edged lance and drove it into the whale's side. The wounded animal's tail flipped upward and then it dove deep into the sea. The tremendous splash from its dive nearly swamped the boat.

Then all was quiet. Most of the line had disappeared from the tubs. A sperm whale is able to stay underwater for a half hour or more, so the men waited in the rain for nearly a quarter of an hour, not knowing what to expect.

At the end of that time the whale shot back to the surface. It was still strong and full of fight. Once more it pulled the boat behind it as it set off in a circle. The men kept the harpoon line tight, hoping to tire the whale.

The whale towed the boat for two miles, uncoiling all of the line. Sometimes when the whale dove, it pulled the bow of the boat completely underwater. Water poured into the little boat, and the men bailed frantically to keep afloat.

The rain clouds disappeared and the sun came out. Two

other whaleboats came alongside to help. The crews tied their lines to the harpoon line in Murphy's boat, but the whale never slowed its pace as it pulled all three boats behind it.

Several more times the boats got close to the whale when it stopped to rest. The men stabbed it with their long lances. But each time the whale dove with a splash, drenching the men and almost upsetting the boat.

It was late in the afternoon when the whalers finally put an end to the battle. One of the boats rowed back to the *Daisy* to get a gun that shot a small bomb.

"A bomb was shot into the whale's lungs, where it exploded with a muffled crack," Murphy wrote afterward. "In his leap, he half filled our boat with water for the last time, but he no longer had the breath to dive. His spout, formerly so thin and white reflecting tiny rainbows in the rays of the low sun, now became first pink and then crimson."

One of the whalemen in the boat watched the bloody spout and turned to the others. "His chimney's on fire!" he shouted with a scornful laugh. The whale died after fighting the harpoons, lances, and bomb for nine hours. The boats towed the dead whale back to the *Daisy*. The next morning the huge carcass was cut up and the blubber —layers of fat—thrown into iron pots on deck where it was boiled down to oil.

The *Daisy* sailed on through the soft, windless days of

the tropics. Then, as it neared the tip of South America, the weather changed. Fierce winds tore at the little ship's sails and blasts of cold air warned the crew that they were coming into the polar seas that ring the South Pole. One day Murphy saw an enormous form on the horizon— high walls of emerald green rising to a gleaming white tip. This was his first sight of an iceberg, taking on color in the Antarctic light.

There was a change in the life around the ship too. Murphy saw thousands of birds—from tiny petrels to giant albatrosses. Some of the birds flew aboard ship, where helpful members of the crew captured them so that Murphy could examine them at close range.

And as the numbers of birds increased, so did the whales. The crew was busy now launching the whaleboats, harpooning whales, and working feverishly to boil down the blubber and store the precious oil in casks or barrels belowdecks. Often sharks, excited by the scent of blood, ripped away chunks of flesh from the whale carcasses that were tied to the ship.

The *Daisy* reached the southern limits of the Atlantic Ocean, close to where it met the Antarctic. It was clear that those cold waters were rich in food. Birds and whales of all kinds gathered there to feed. Murphy climbed the mainmast and got a bird's-eye view of whales spread across the sea. Sometimes he looked down on a whale that

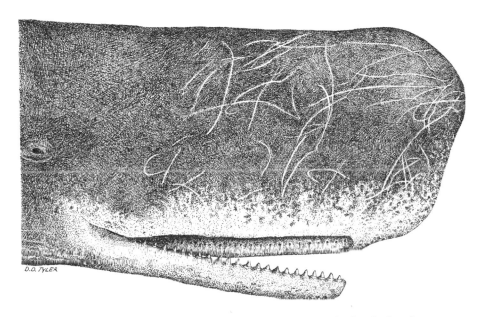

Head of a sperm whale. The largest of the toothed whales has teeth in the lower jaw, while the upper jaw has sockets.

surfaced alongside the ship, spouting as its broad back broke the water. "The slit of the blowholes opened like a pair of lips," he wrote, "and a slight shower of spray accompanied a gentle puff."

While he was aboard the *Daisy*, Murphy lived with men whose business was killing whales. When they saw a whale, their only thought was to stick a harpoon into it, then drag it back to the ship to boil it down into oil. But as Murphy watched these giant mammals rolling on the surface and splashing with their flippers and flukes, he began to see them in a different way. He recognized their intelligence.

"Whatever dim ideas were in them were quite unfishlike," he wrote in his *Logbook*. "These whales undoubtedly saw us, probably recognized us as another kind of living creature, and may have believed that they were playing with us instead of merely for us. What a pity that unwieldy circumstances prevent us from becoming as well acquainted with the personalities of whales as we have, for example, with those of sea lions that learn to toss balls and ride horseback! I suspect that a whale's desire to become chummy and companionable might astonish the world."

But the young scientist was now sailing into a world that was even more intent on killing. The crew of the *Daisy* saw land at last. Through sleet and mist they made out the treeless mountains of South Georgia Island.

This island, a little more than a hundred miles long, lies in the South Atlantic twelve hundred miles east of the tip of South America. The *Daisy*'s crew surely thought they had reached the end of the world. Although it was summer, ice and snow covered the higher ground. No flowering plants grow any farther south in the world than there.

Yet Murphy found a busy industry on this bleak island. Steamships sailed in and out of the bays, hunting whales, killing them with powerful guns that shot harpoons, and towing them back to the island. Factories had been built on the island to strip the whales of the parts that people wanted. The rest was left to rot. No whales, no matter how large or fast, escaped this industry that depended on all kinds of new inventions.

When the *Daisy* entered a bay, Murphy smelled the strong odor of rotting flesh. The smells and sights of the killing were all around him.

"The whole shoreline of the bay proved to be lined for miles with the bones of whales, mostly humpbacks," Bob Murphy wrote in *Logbook for Grace*. "Spinal columns, loose vertebrae, ribs and jaws were piled in heaps along the waterline. And it was easy to count a hundred huge skulls within a stone's throw. This district is an enormous graveyard of whales, yet no one can guess how many thousands of carcasses have been taken out to sea by the tide, and so have sunk their skeletons in the deep."

In 1912 this young scientist saw the beginning of a slaughter that was to become greater than anything that had gone before.

3
THE GREAT SLAUGHTER

It took many centuries to develop a modern whaling industry like that which Robert Cushman Murphy found at South Georgia Island.

Men have hunted whales for several thousand years. The imaginations of early people must have been stirred by these "monsters of the deep" that sometimes drifted up on beaches to die. One carcass would keep a whole village in meat for a long time. Indians, Eskimos, and Vikings hunted small whales close to shore, paddling after them in dugout canoes or boats made of animal skins. It was dangerous work in their frail boats. They probably didn't kill very many whales.

The first famous whalers of fairly recent times were the Basque people of northern Spain. About a thousand years ago they began to build ships to hunt whales in the

Bay of Biscay. They killed only a few each year. But after hundreds of years they finally killed most of the whales in the bay.

The Basques made one very important discovery: they learned to cut up the dead whale at sea, boiling the blubber on shipboard, rather than tow the entire carcass back to shore. This saved time and enabled them to catch more whales.

Soon the people of many countries were building whaling ships. At first they hunted the whales only for food. But the world was changing. People began to want whale oil for lamps and smokeless candles. They also wanted the baleen or "whalebone" for brushes, utensils, and other products.

By the 1800s most of the countries of northern Europe, as well as the United States, had whaling fleets. The art of "catching" a whale that was developed by ancient people had not changed. The idea is simply to get close enough to a whale to plunge a harpoon, with a line attached to the boat, into its body. Other aspects of whaling have changed, including the means of putting the harpoon into the whale—but the harpoon and line remain the essential tool for the catch.

Robert Cushman Murphy sailed aboard a whaling ship that was very much the same as those used by whalers for nearly two hundred years. There was no machinery, no radio, and no means of refrigeration. The ship was driven by the wind, and all the work aboard—even that of killing, cutting, and boiling—was done by hand and with primitive tools.

As we have seen, whalers on ships like the *Daisy* could capture only certain kinds of whales. Some of the larger whales were too fast and large for the old sailing ships. Even if the crew managed to kill one, it sank to the bottom almost at once.

But whalers learned that several kinds of whales were wrapped so thickly in layers of blubber that they floated on the ocean's surface even after they had been killed. One kind of whale—the bowhead—has a layer of blubber almost two feet thick. Another kind is still known to us by the name the old whaling men gave it—the right whale. For them, it was the "right" whale to kill because it floated when it died and could be towed to the ship.

Murphy described the dangerous and tiring work of killing a whale. But the whalers still had a long day's work ahead of them once they got a dead whale in tow. When the whale had been tied to the ship's side, the crew gathered for the "cutting-in." Strips of blubber were cut from the whale with sharp, long-handled tools called blubber spades. Large iron hooks that weighed a hundred pounds were fastened into the blubber and used to tear off the strips, which were then hoisted on deck.

The right whale, blowing.

Whale Watch

As the men peeled the blubber from the whale, schools of sharks often attacked the carcass. They tried to get at the meat beneath the blubber. Sharks even leaped onto a dead whale's back, where the men killed them with their blubber spades. Aboard ship other men cut up the blubber strips with short-handled spades. The decks of the rocking ship were awash in grease and blood.

Two enormous iron pots, standing on bricks, were set boiling on the forward deck. Water was continually splashed across the deck to keep it from catching fire. The thin strips of blubber were soon boiled down to a golden oil. What was left of the strips was by then cooked to shriveled brown scraps. The scraps were used as fuel to keep the fire going, so that the blubber was really boiled by blubber itself. The oil was put into cooling tanks and later stored in casks belowdecks. The largest whales that the old sailing ships were able to catch usually produced about forty barrels of oil.

By the end of the nineteenth century many of the whales hunted by the old sailing ships were fast disappearing from the oceans. The ships had to sail ever farther from their home ports to find whales they could kill. Sometimes the ships that sailed from Nantucket, New Bedford, and other New England ports were gone for two years or more. Many whaling men lost their lives when their ships sank in fierce storms at the ends of the earth, or whales that they had harpooned smashed their small boats. *Moby Dick*, perhaps the greatest novel ever written by an American, is Herman Melville's story about a whaling voyage to the South Pacific.

But even at the time that *Moby Dick* was being published in 1851, the whaling industry was beginning to change. A Norwegian named Sven Foyn invented a cannon that shot harpoons. It was a deadly weapon. The harpoon had a tip that held many sharp barbs and a shell filled with gunpowder. When the cannon shot the harpoon into a whale, the barbs flew open like an umbrella. It was almost impossible for a whale to pull the tip free from its flesh. At the same time a bomb exploded inside the whale.

The Norwegians also developed small steamboats called whale catchers that had a cannon mounted in the bow of the boat. These boats could travel faster than sailing ships and they could keep up with the large whales—but there was still a big problem to solve. Even if the whale catchers could now kill the large whale, how could they keep the dead giants from sinking?

The Norwegians solved that by inventing a hollow lance. This lance was attached to a hose. When a whale was killed, a member of the crew pushed the hollow lance into its belly and pumped it up like a balloon with compressed air from tanks on the ship. The air-filled whale floated until the crew stripped it of its blubber.

Soon the Norwegians became the leading whalers in

the world. Along with other countries that copied their inventions, they killed most of the whales in the northern oceans. The United States, with its fleet of old sailing ships, could not match them.

Whaling ships at the beginning of the twentieth century were not large enough to hold the oil and other products taken from whales. So wherever the Norwegians and other whalers went to hunt them, they began to build whaling stations on the shore. Ships towed dead whales back to factories at these stations. There the big animals were cut up and prepared for various products. There were eighteen whaling stations on the shores of Newfoundland alone in 1904. These factories received twelve hundred large whales a year.

It wasn't long before the factories in the North Atlantic were running out of whales. Even the Norwegians could not find enough left in the ocean. But for some years other Norwegian ships had traveled into the southern oceans near the Antarctic to hunt seals. A Norwegian who made trips to the Antarctic was Captain Carl Anton Larsen. He noticed there were thousands of large whales near South Georgia and other islands in those cold seas.

Until about the year 1900 the blue whales, fin whales, and other great whales of the southern oceans lived in a watery Garden of Eden. They had few enemies in the sea and all the food they needed. The oceans of the earth differ from the continents because the coldest regions are the richest in living things. We know that on land it is the warmest parts—great tropical jungles near the equator—where plants and animals usually grow in vast numbers. But the oceans near the equator are poor in their production of life. Some scientists call these warm regions "biological deserts" because they support so little life.

The cold seas near the poles are entirely different. Cold water absorbs oxygen and other elements needed for life much more readily than does warm water. Also, these seas are generally stormy. The life-giving elements called nutrients are continually being churned up and sent to the ocean's surface, so the tiny animals on which seabirds and the great whales feed are found in enormous quantities.

Some of the coldest currents in the world flow up from the Antarctic past South Georgia Island. The sea off South Georgia is alive with tiny, shrimplike animals called krill; seabirds and whales gather there to feed on them. Whales lived there in peace, with hardly any more contact with people than if they were dinosaurs.

After Captain Larsen noticed the whales around South Georgia, he raised money to form a company and build a whaling station on the shore. It was there that Robert Cushman Murphy met Captain Larsen in 1912. On the island by that time were seven different whaling stations

A bowhead whale. The head is one third the size of the body, and the upper jaw is highly arched—hence its name.

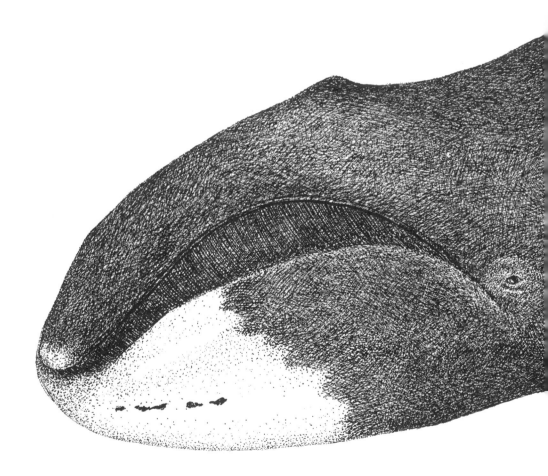

owned by the Norwegians and the British. The whales'
Garden of Eden had become a battleground.

When Murphy first sailed into those waters, he heard
not only the cries of seabirds but the booming of cannons
on the little whale catchers that seemed everywhere
around the island.

"The day before yesterday 60 whales were received at
the factory here," Murphy wrote in his *Logbook*. "Carcasses lay afloat in addition to those lying side by side on
the shore. Now they are all gone except for two or three
still in the factory. The rest are already oil and fertilizer."

The Norwegian factories at South Georgia were mar-
keting whale products all over the world. Whale oil was
no longer needed for lighting people's houses. The inven-
tion of the electric light and the discovery of oil wells on
land had pushed whale oil out of that market. But whale
oil was in great demand for lubricating machinery. Industry also used oil and other parts of whales to make
fertilizer, cosmetics, margarine, feed for animals, and
even dynamite.

The great whales never had a chance. The Norwegians
and other whalers used the complicated machinery of the
time to make it easier to kill them. They hunted whales
across the southern oceans. The ships stopped the hunt
only to tow the carcasses back to whaling stations.

Even that brief resting time for the whales came to an

end in 1922. In that year the Norwegians built the first factory ship. In one sense, this development meant a return to the old days before whaling stations, when the whale was cut up aboard ship. But the new factory ship was much more efficient. It looked like a large freighter. It had a wide hole with a great door in the stern, and modern machinery pulled the whale up into the heart of the ship, which was fitted out like a slaughterhouse. Workers quickly cut up the whale and prepared the various products, while the little steam whale catchers went right back to the business of killing. All the large whales were in danger, wherever they swam and fed.

4
WHAT IS A WHALE?

There are about eighty-five different kinds—or species—of whales in the world's oceans. Most whales have teeth. They are called the toothed whales and, aside from the sperm whale, they are the smaller kinds such as the killer whale, the dolphins, and the porpoises. The other ten species, called the baleen or whalebone whales, are toothless and generally very large.

A fin whale used to be a familiar sight in the cold waters near South Georgia Island. Picture a calm day at sea. The only living things in sight are seabirds, circling low over the water as if they knew something was going to happen. Suddenly the water's surface is broken by a dark, rounded form, looking like a mountain being pushed up from the ocean depths.

The huge form is the back of a fin whale. Only part of

the back shows as the whale begins to come up for air. It is the forward part of the whale, the top of the head where the whale's nostrils are placed, allowing it to breathe while continuing to swim partly underwater. The valves of the nostrils or blowholes open and the whale "blows"—a loud snort as it comes to the surface, sending a dense spout into the air. The explosive spout is followed by a *slurp* as the great whale sucks in air before going under again.

The blowholes snap shut. The whale seems to be doing a slow cartwheel as it dives, the blowholes disappearing and the rest of the back revealing itself in a gentle arc. The fin from which the whale takes its name—and which is set far back on its body—follows the long unbroken stretch of back and the whale disappears. All that is visible on the surface are two "footprints"—patches of swirling water created by the whale's flukes as it pushes itself down into the sea.

The fin whale is feeding just below the surface. Its powerful flukes pump slowly up and down, pushing the whale easily through the water. The flippers on each side of the dark body hardly move. The whale extends them now and then just to keep itself balanced as it swims along. The streamlined, hairless body slides through the water without disturbing it. As a scientist has written, "Apparently the outer layers of a whale—skin, blubber,

and the immediate underlying areas of connective tissue
—have the capacity to simulate fluids in motion, almost
as if they were themselves a liquid substance."

Ahead of the whale drifts a mass of krill. The whale
pumps its flukes up and down and moves faster. As it
comes close to the little shrimplike animals, it rolls over
slightly on one side. Like the other baleen whales, the fin
whale is ready to feed in a remarkable way. It opens its
tremendous mouth. The throat of the fin whale is lined
with hundreds of grooves running from the mouth toward the belly. Its throat is really pleated like a fan that
is partly closed. As the water rushes into its open mouth,
the pressure flattens out the grooves so that the mouth
bulges much larger than its natural size.

The whale bursts into the middle of the drifting krill,
and they flow with the water into its wide mouth. When
the mouth is full it holds hundreds of pounds of krill. The
whale closes its mouth, and the krill are trapped.

Now we see what makes the baleen whales different
from other mammals. The fin whale's mouth is filled not
with teeth but with baleen, or whalebone. Baleen isn't
teeth, or bone either. It is two rows of horny plates with
hairlike fringes that hang from the roof of the mouth.
It looks like a thick mustache. It is made of the same
substance that makes our hair and fingernails.

When the whale is ready to swallow, it lifts its enor-

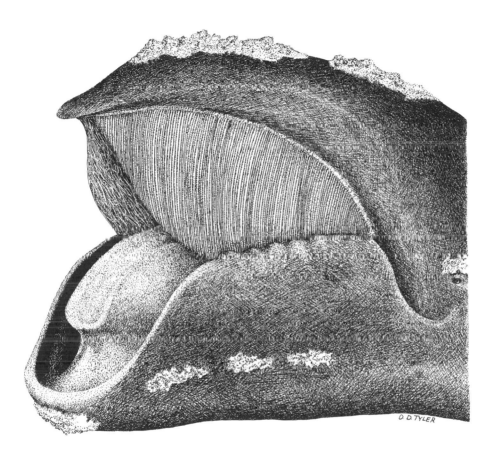

Baleen of the right whale.

mous flabby tongue, which in some species is nearly as big as an elephant. The tongue pushes the mouthful of water toward the sides of the mouth and through the thick mass of baleen. The krill are strained out of the water and caught in the hairlike baleen while the water is squirted out of the sides of the whale's mouth. The whale gulps and the krill disappear down its gullet.

The fin whale, which sometimes weighs as much as seventy tons, is the second largest creature that has ever lived on earth. The only creature that is larger is its close relative, the blue whale. Even the dinosaurs never grew as large.

Blue whales have almost followed the dinosaurs, as the modern whaling fleets pushed them to the edge of extinction. Scientists have told us more about the fin whales because there are more of them around to study. The blue whales have grown as long as a hundred feet and reached a weight of over a hundred tons—as much as thirty full-grown elephants!

Creatures so large can live only in the sea. The oceans cover nearly three-fourths of our planet and are the whales' element, just as the air is the element of birds and butterflies.

It was not always so. The ancestors of whales were not fish, but mammals that lived on land. They had legs and fur just like a buffalo or a moose.

But something happened to drive these mammals to the

sea. We know that there are many mammals that find it easier to live in and around the water. Beavers and musk-rats are excellent swimmers and build their homes in the water. Seals have gone even further, living much of their lives in the sea. They have kept their fur and come to shore to give birth and raise their young. In the seals' flippers we can see the remains of what once were legs.

But the whales went all the way. They spend their entire lives in the world's vast oceans. They feed and sleep in the ocean and even give birth there. They never pull themselves up onto a rock to sun themselves as seals do. The front legs of whales gradually turned into flip-pers. Their hind legs, for which they had no use in the water, gradually faded away. The big job of pushing a whale along has been taken over by its tail with the two flat fins called flukes. Fish swim by moving their tails from side to side—whales pump their tails up and down.

Whales even lost their fur. Some still show a few hairs around their lips or head, but to keep warm in icy regions of the ocean, whales have grown a thick layer of fatty, oily blubber just under the skin. Blubber is not soft like jelly, but very firm—"like a thick side of well-cured bacon," a scientist says.

A whale that is wrapped in its thick coat of blubber is not bothered by cold weather, even in the Antarctic. In fact, the blubber gives a whale so much protection that the heat of its body cannot escape very easily. When a whale dies, the heat stays in the body. If the blubber is not stripped away at once, its flesh will cook.

Life in the ocean caused other changes in a whale's body:

• Its eyes grew small because it has little need to see very far in the ocean where the light is poor.

• Its ears disappeared from the outside of its head. Sound travels much better in water than in air, and so the whale is still able to hear very well with ears that are tucked away inside its head.

• Its nostrils "migrated" to the top of its head. In that way, a whale can still keep its head mostly underwater and look for food while only the blowholes remain above water for breathing.

Whales found the oceans to be a good place to live. There was plenty of food and few enemies. Because their coat of blubber made it easy for them to float, it didn't matter how heavy they grew. Animals on land could not grow so heavy because their legs would not be able to hold them up. They would have a hard time moving around to find food and escape their enemies. They would be helpless. But whales just ate and ate and grew into the largest creatures that ever lived. They can move through the water with hardly any effort at all.

The whole world became the whale's home because the oceans go completely around the earth. Protected by their thick blubber, whales can wander anywhere. There are

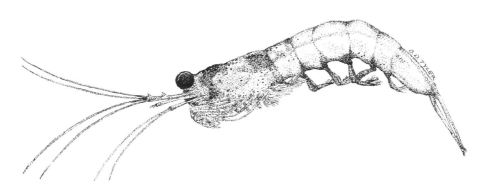

Krill. These animals grow to be no longer than three inches. A female is capable of laying 11,000 eggs.

no deserts to cross, no high mountains or thick jungles to bar their way. Whales filled all the seas.

Of course, whales do not swim thousands of miles just for the sake of change. Like most other animals, they move about in search of food. During the summers near the North Pole and the South Pole, daylight never ends, and the tiny plants which are the base of all food chains grow well in so much light. Small sea animals feed on the plants, and the whales come to spend the summer feeding on the small sea animals. As summer and daylight fade, the whales swim off to warmer regions where they mate and have their calves.

The gray whale is a baleen whale like the fin whale. At the end of the summer feeding in the Arctic seas, it swims thousands of miles south along the Pacific Coast to Mexico's Baja California, where it gives birth to its young.

Millions of years ago the whales split into two main

groups. One group learned to feed on the great masses of krill and other tiny animals that drift near the ocean's surface. They didn't need sharp teeth. They simply opened their mouths and swallowed. Scientists, in fact, sometimes call these whales "gulpers." The dense mustaches of baleen that strain the food out of the water inside their mouths are more useful to them than teeth.

But most of the whales kept their teeth. They feed not in large mouthfuls but on one animal at a time. The sperm whale eats fish of many kinds—mostly squid or octopus. It seizes the fish with its teeth and then swallows it whole.

While the baleen whales seldom dive very deep because they find most of their food close to the surface, sperm whales are excellent divers. They chase fish deep into the ocean and stay underwater for half an hour and sometimes for an hour. They have been found caught in telephone cables more than half a mile down on the ocean floor. A sperm whale can hold its breath and can even slow down its heartbeat so it has no need to breathe for long periods of time.

There is great variety even among the toothed whales. They differ in size from the sperm whale, which grows anywhere from thirty-five to sixty feet long, to some of the dolphins and porpoises, which may be only five or six feet long.

One of the toothed whales is the narwhal, a small whale

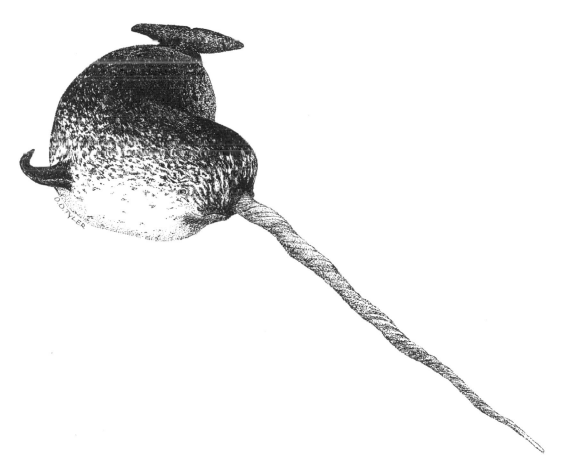

Narwhal.

of the Arctic seas that has a tooth sticking out of its upper jaw like a spear. This tooth is eight feet long. Sometimes in ancient days people found a narwhal's tooth washed up on shore. They could not figure out what strange beast grew such a "horn." They made up a deerlike animal called the unicorn that had only one horn—a long, straight horn that sprang from the center of its head. If anyone doubted that there really was such an animal, these people simply pointed to the long tooth and asked, "What other animal would have such a horn?" It was a long time before people found out that this "horn" was the tooth of a whale that lives in the Arctic.

Perhaps the most feared members of the whale family are the killer whales. They are beautiful animals, dark with white patterns, a white oval face patch, and a tall fin on the back that reminds some people of a shark's fin. They have sharp teeth and powerful jaws. They travel in packs, hunting seals, walruses, penguins, and occasionally other whales. But killer whales are not the villains that people sometimes suppose them to be.

Scientists tell us that killer whales are just large dolphins. Indeed, all of the toothed whales except the sperm whale are called dolphins or porpoises, even such large ones as the killer, pilot, and white whales. There are about seventy-five kinds in all. Even scientists seem to be confused about the difference between dolphins and porpoises. Some say that any toothed whale that has a beak-like snout is a dolphin, and the rest are porpoises. But no one is really clear about the differences. Scientists, just like the rest of us, now say that any of these smaller whales can be called either dolphins or porpoises. The two words mean the same thing.

Fin whales once gathered in large numbers two or three times a year, whole families coming together until there were three hundred or more whales in one place. Young whales found mates at these meeting places. An old-time whaling captain recalled his visits to lagoons in Baja California, where whales came to give birth, "huddled together so thickly that it was difficult for a boat to cross the water without coming in contact with them."

There were once a half million fin whales living in Antarctic waters. There are now perhaps eighty thousand. During the 1920s there may have been two hundred thousand blue whales in the Antarctic. Now a blue whale is hard to find. There are so few left that single male blue whales may wander the oceans for years looking for a female. Thousands of miles now separate whales which once came together in great numbers. Scientists wonder if these whales will be able to find each other often enough to mate and keep their species from dying out once and for all.

For the great whales that are left, the ocean has become a vast, empty world.

5

THE FACTORY SHIP

The factory ship is a floating industrial city. Seamen, helicopter pilots, butchers, blacksmiths, sonar technicians, cooks, and chemists all live and work together on board. It is their job to take the great whales and turn them into oil, meat, pet food, and cosmetics.

When the factory ships steamed into the Antarctic, the great whales began to disappear. The ships were just too good at their job. The Japanese, who learned from the Norwegians, built modern factory ships and became the best whale killers in the world. The Russians also built a large fleet of whaling ships.

Like every successful industry, whaling made good use of new technology. The boats that chased whales at one time were powered by sails and oars. Later the Norwegians used steam whale catchers. The modern catcher ships are driven by diesel engines. They are noisier than the old-fashioned boats and often frighten the whales. But that doesn't make any difference—they are so fast that they chase the whales and tire them out so the big mammals become easier to kill.

In the old days on whaling ships, a sailor climbed the mast to look for whales. Modern whaling fleets keep men on lookout, but they also have many other ways to find whales. Some factory ships carry a helicopter aboard. Every day it is flown out over the ocean to help the whale catchers look for whales. The catcher ships also carry sonar machines. These machines send sound waves into the water. When the sound waves strike a large object underwater, they "bounce" back to the ship. The machines are so sensitive that they can tell whether the object is a whale or simply floating ice.

When a whale is sighted, the catcher ship begins the chase. The whale dives, leaving on the sea the big, swirling patches created by its flukes. The gunner takes his place at his harpoon gun in the bow. He makes a guess where and when the whale will return to the surface to breathe. The man at the wheel steers the boat to where the gunner tells him.

There is a commotion in the water just ahead. A great length of dark back breaks the water's surface and the gunner sees a baleen whale's spout. He directs the ship

A modern harpoon gun.

close to the whale. As it begins to dive, the gunner pulls the trigger and fires a harpoon into the whale's back.

There is a muffled roar and a burst of smoke as the bomb in the harpoon's nose explodes inside the whale. A cloud of bright red blood spreads across the water's surface.

The wounded whale leaps forward and begins to dive. But it is held tightly by the harpoon line that is fastened to the ship. If the whale doesn't die quickly, the gunner fires another harpoon into it. The whale rolls over, belly up, and drifts quietly on the crimson sea.

A doctor, who sailed abroad a modern whaling ship, has this to say:

"The present-day hunting harpoon is a horrible 150-pound weapon carrying an explosive head which bursts generally in the whale's intestines, and the sight of one of these creatures pouring blood and gasping along on the surface, towing a 100-ton catching vessel by a heavy harpoon rope, is pitiful. So often an hour or more of torture is inflicted before the agony ends in death. I have experienced a case of five hours and nine harpoons needed to kill one mother blue whale. If we could imagine a horse having two or three explosive spears driven into it, and then made to drag a heavy butcher's truck while blood poured over the roadway until the animal collapsed an hour or more later, we should have some idea of what a whale goes through."

A winch on the catcher ship pulls the dead whale alongside. The gunner thrusts the long hollow lance into its belly and pumps air into it to keep it afloat. The crew also plants a long pole with a flag on it in the whale's body, and sometimes a radar buoy. Then the whale catcher cuts the whale loose and leaves in search of other whales. Another, smaller boat called the buoy boat comes along later and is able to find the whale's floating carcass because of the flag and radar buoy. This boat finds all of the whales killed by the catcher ships and tows them back to the factory ship.

The many experts aboard the factory ship work in shifts to keep the factory going twenty-four hours a day. Blacksmiths keep the tools in working condition and carpenters make needed equipment. Workers have recreation rooms in which to spend their time, and there is a well-equipped hospital aboard.

When the buoy ship comes into sight, trailing its cluster of dead whales, the workers are ready. The huge door at the ship's stern opens. One by one the carcasses, tail first, are pulled by winches up the wide, sloping ramp into the ship. Workers called flensers go to work on the carcass at once. They make deep cuts in the whale blubber, then run a wire through the blubber to a powerful winch. A scientist who has watched this job says that the winch "peels the blubber off in enormous strips, just like peeling a huge banana, with a sound like the tearing of a million sheets of paper."

The workers cut the blubber into smaller pieces and drop it to a deck below where other workers grind it up and put it into boilers. The whale's flesh is cut up and frozen, or ground into meat meal. The bones are sawed up and boiled for their oil. The guts are made into pet food or thrown into the sea.

The Factory Ship

Whale oil is the most important product to be made on European factory ships. Japanese people, however, eat whale meat, and this product gets the most attention on their ships. Japanese ships even buy meat from some European factory ships. But whatever the product—oil or meat—a great deal of care goes into storing it so it will not spoil. Chemists examine the products on board to make sure their quality is good and that they remain free from contamination. Engineers continually check the big refrigerators and other storage equipment to see that they are running properly.

And so, day after day, year after year, the world's great whales have been turned into products for people. The whalers did not leave enough whales to mate and restore the population of some species. The attack on the blue whale, the largest creature of all, was the most thorough. During the 1930–1931 season, whalers killed more than twenty-five thousand blue whales in the Antarctic alone. The killing went on so that by the 1964–1965 season, the whalers could find only twenty blue whales to kill.

As the blue whale disappeared, the whalers began to hunt other kinds. Fin whales, the second largest, were next. As they became scarce, smaller baleen whales such as the Minke whales were killed in great numbers. These whales, which grow to be fifteen to thirty feet long, got their name from an old whaling captain named Minke

The blue whale.

who mistook one for a blue whale! After that, his friends called these whales after him.

The whales got a brief rest during World War II, because most of the Japanese whaling ships were sunk. After the war the United States government helped to rebuild the shattered Japanese nation and supplied it with ships to put it back into the whaling business. The Japanese and the Russians spent an enormous amount of money building up their fleets.

Those two countries once more became the leading whalers in the world. They hunted whales relentlessly in the North Pacific Ocean as well as in the Antarctic. Their modern factory ships, large, expensive, and efficient, made killing whales easier than it had ever been before. Scientists say that during the last fifty years the industry has killed more than two million whales.

6

THE DEATH
OF A WHALE

For some years a writer and naturalist named Farley
Mowat lived with his wife, Claire, in the fishing village of
Burgeo on the south coast of Newfoundland. There he
had the kind of experience that very few people have had
with a whale. It ended in the death of a single whale at a
time when many thousands were being killed all over
the world. But Farley Mowat had a special regard for
whales. The book he wrote about the experience, *A Whale
for the Killing*, helped a great many other people to start
thinking about whales in a new way.

An old fisherman in Burgeo told Mowat how the waters
off the coast used to be filled with whales. The old man
had fished for herring right alongside the whales. But
then the whaling ships came to those waters. The whalers
built shore stations where the big carcasses were towed

and cut up. Few whales were seen off Burgeo by the time Farley and Claire Mowat came to live there.

Sometimes small family groups of fin whales were seen near Burgeo in winter when they came to feed on herring. The Mowats got great pleasure from watching the whales feeding in a lonely cove near their home. Once they flew in a small plane over a family of whales swimming just below the surface. They marveled at the graceful movement of the whales through the water. "It's like watching a fantastic ballet," Claire Mowat said. "They aren't swimming through the water—they're dancing through it!"

One day after a big storm in January an astonishing thing happened. Near Burgeo there was a little saltwater pond, partly cut off from the sea by rocks. Somehow a large female fin whale got over the rocks and into the pond. The storm had been fierce, the tide high, and the whale had probably been chasing a school of herring. When the whale finished feeding in the pond, the storm was over and she was trapped.

Word that a giant whale was trapped in the pond quickly spread through the town. For some reason several men in the town decided it would be great fun to go to the pond and shoot at the whale.

"The five men wasted no time," Mowat wrote in his book. "Some dropped to their knees levering shells into their rifles as they did so. Others stood where they were and hurriedly took aim. The crash of rifle fire began to echo from the cliffs enclosing the pond and, as an undertone, there came the flat satisfying *thunk* of bullets striking home in living flesh. After an hour the men had exhausted their supply of shells."

But the men returned with more ammunition the next day. They fired hundreds of bullets into the thick blubber of the frightened whale. Her skin was scarred with bullet holes but she did not seem to be seriously hurt. A curious part of the incident was that another large whale, surely her mate, was often seen in the ocean near the entrance to the little cove, keeping the trapped whale company. Sometimes it seemed as if the big whale outside was trying to drive schools of herring into the cove for his mate to eat.

Farley Mowat was wild with anger when he learned that men were shooting at the trapped whale. He made up his mind to help her. He arranged to have a Royal Canadian Police officer patrol the cove to keep people from shooting at her or chasing her around the shallow little pond in their motorboats. Many of the townspeople, even some of his old friends, were angry with Mowat for trying to help the whale. They believed they had a right to shoot at it if they wanted to.

Mowat knew that time was short. Even if the whale

was not killed by the high-powered rifles, she might soon die of hunger. He hired some local fishermen to help him drive schools of herring into the cove. He made long-distance telephone calls all over the United States and Canada to try to get help for the whale.

The Newfoundland government promised to send a big fishing boat to help, but it did not arrive in time. Newspapers all over the world carried stories about the trapped whale and Mowat's attempt to help it. People who had never given a second thought to the slaughter of two million whales now were in sympathy with this one fin whale as she fought for her life.

Mowat hoped to keep her alive until another high tide might help to float her over the rocks and back into the sea. Every day he and a fisherman friend went into the cove to stay with her. Her mate was always waiting just outside the cove.

One day when Mowat rowed across the cove the great whale swam slowly under his boat. For the first time he heard her voice. "It was a long, low, sonorous moan with unearthly overtones in a higher pitch," he wrote later. "It was unbelievably weird and bore no affinity with any sound I have heard from any other living thing. It was a voice not of the world we know."

Mowat wrote that he will always believe that this trapped creature had tried to communicate with him—to reach out across the space that separates two species.

The Death of a Whale

He failed, yet it was not a total failure. "So long as I live I shall hear the echoes of that haunting cry," he went on. "And they will remind me that life itself—not *human* life—is the ultimate miracle upon this earth. I will hear those echoes even if the day should come when none of her nation is left alive in the desecrated seas, and the voices of the great whales have been silenced forever."

Mowat lost his struggle to keep the whale alive. He began to notice ugly bumps all over her back where the bullets had smashed into her. Day by day the swellings grew larger. She began to spend more time floating on the surface of the little cove, while her spout grew weaker. Pus dripped from the sores that covered her great body.

Toward the end the whale could no longer keep herself afloat. Several times she dragged her huge body up on the beach. Each time she rested her head on the rocks, then pushed off again. Mowat heard her cry only once more.

"It was the most desolate cry I have ever heard," he wrote in his book. He knew that this was her leave-taking. The next day she drowned, sinking to the bottom of the little cove, too weak to push herself back to the surface to breathe. "It was dark, and there was none to know that I was weeping," Mowat wrote, "weeping not just for the whale that died but because the fragile link between her race and mine was severed."

Farley Mowat was not alone in his despair. For some

61

time other people here and there around the world were coming to believe that all the whales would be killed before humanity established any link with them at all. Whales breed very slowly. Some, like the blue whales, give birth to a single calf every two years. Whales were being killed much faster than they could reproduce.

Were there any attempts to put limits on the killing of whales? There were—but this attempt was controlled by the whaling industry itself. The industry made people believe that something was being done to help whales, but the whalers were really too greedy to put any effective limits on the killing—the whales continued to disappear.

As long ago as 1931 many of the world's whaling nations met in Geneva, Switzerland, to talk about the disappearance of whales. Since most of the people there made their money by killing whales, they did not come to the meeting out of sympathy for them. They came because they were worried that the whales would become extinct and the whaling companies would go out of business.

After several years of talking about it, the whalers agreed to protect two species—the right whales and the bowhead whales. This was not such an unselfish agreement as it sounds. Both species had been hunted relent-

Fin whale, diving.

lessly for years and they were nearly extinct anyway. There were so few of them left and they were so hard to find that it was no longer worth the whalers' time to hunt them. The whalers also agreed not to kill females of any species when they were accompanied by a calf. Even these few agreements did not amount to much. Several leading whaling nations, such as Japan, did not sign the treaty.

Even greater slaughter lay just ahead. After World War II most whaling nations realized that the danger of extinction was very real, so they formed the International Whaling Commission in 1946. The commission's charter said:

"The history of whaling has seen overfishing of one area after another and of one species of whale after another to such a degree that it is essential to protect all species of whales from further overfishing."

The whalers, as you see, thought of whales as simply big "fish." Then the charter went on to say that the commission's purpose was "the orderly development of the whaling industry." The whalers, however, were making so much money that they were in no hurry to act—it was three years before they held their first meeting.

Scientists were appointed to give advice to the other members of the commission. The scientists warned that there would soon be very few whales left to kill. They tried to get the commission members to run the industry properly by killing only as many whales as the whales themselves could replace through births. In that way the population would not decline. Scientists called this plan a "sustained yield."

The scientists warned the other members about the blue whale in particular. They reported that it was disappearing rapidly. But the whaling nations paid no attention, and went right on killing blue whales just like the other species. It took the commission eighteen years to stop the killing of blue whales. By then, as was the case with the right and bowhead whales, blue whales were so scarce that it wasn't worthwhile hunting them anymore.

Why did the International Whaling Commission, which was supposed to put limits on the killing, go on destroying its own industry? Certainly the commission members behaved stupidly. But there were other reasons that tell us something about the way in which people act and why it is difficult to save any endangered animals.

The whaling industry had changed radically after World War II. The nations that had invested so much money in the ships and equipment wanted to earn the money back as quickly as possible. They could do that only by killing every whale in sight.

Part of the trouble also lay with the commission itself. Each of the world's nations fiercely protects its own interests. No nation would join such an organization if its people thought it would have to do what other nations told it to. So the charter of the International Whaling Commission made it difficult to get anything done. A simple majority vote on any question was not enough. Three-quarters of all the nations on the commission had to agree to any proposal before it became a fact. Even if three-quarters agreed, any nation could come back within ninety days and say it would not agree to obey the new ruling—and no one could force it to obey.

The case of the blue whale shows how it was almost impossible for the commission to take the needed action. When its own scientists urged the commission members to give the blue whale a chance to build up its population, they refused to agree—because blue whales are the largest animals of all, and yield the most oil and meat. Some nations did not want to stop killing blue whales until they had paid for their modern fleets of ships. The Japanese even invented a new species of whale to get around the scientists' arguments. They said that the blue whales they hunted were different from the others and they called them "pygmy blue whales." This was a trick, but it gave them an excuse to go on hunting blue whales even after the other nations stopped.

For many years the Japanese opposed all limits on the killing of whales. They were supported in the voting by Russia, Norway, Denmark, Iceland, and South Africa.

Those countries all had many whaling ships or factories to pay for.

The United States led the nations that tried to put limits on the killing. Its representatives on the commission argued that quotas should be set for each species— the total number of whales of each species killed should be no higher than the number of calves born to that species. The United States was usually supported by Canada, Great Britain, Australia, France, Mexico, Panama, Brazil, and Argentina.

The commission was a failure even though it was created not to save whales but to save the whaling industry. But because of the shortsightedness of some of its member nations, the commission was unable to do even that. Some of the member nations gave up whaling because it was no longer profitable. They had killed the goose that laid the golden egg. But several other nations —including Japan and Russia—stubbornly opposed rules that might have saved both the whales and their own whaling industries.

But meanwhile, many people in all nations are beginning to agree with Farley Mowat. The great whales are a miracle of life. They deserve a better fate than humanity has so far planned for them.

7
THE BIRTH OF A WHALE

To live in the oceans, the great whales have developed certain habits and bodily functions that are unlike those of other mammals. Whalers use their knowledge about whales in some cases to make killing them easier. But by ignoring or misunderstanding other parts of the whales' lives, they brought about the disaster we see today.

The birth of a whale calf, which is already an enormous animal when it comes into the world, takes a great deal of the mother's strength. Baleen whales are able to give birth only once every two years. Usually one calf is born at a time. Twins are as rare among whales as they are among human beings—about one set of twins for each one hundred pregnancies. For this reason the great whales have not been able to recover from humanity's attacks.

The Birth of a Whale

Baleen whales, as we have seen, find most of their food in the cold seas of the northern and southern polar regions. Animals generally give birth where there is plenty of food for their young. Curiously, this is not possible for the great whales. They travel thousands of miles to give birth in a place where there is little food for either mothers or calves. The mothers, in fact, often carry their food with them.

The story begins once the adult whales have left the feeding grounds in the Arctic or Antarctic. Ice clogs the water, the sun drops below the horizon, and the long polar night comes on. Because there is no sunlight near the poles during the winter, the tiny creatures on which the whales feed do not multiply.

Yet the whales have eaten enormous amounts of food—tons of it every day—during the four or five months of the polar summer. They store much of this nourishment in their blubber, which is now thick and firm. The whales swim north into warmer waters. They will eat very little during the coming months. Like a camel that can go without water for a long time in the desert, the baleen whales can live partly on their own blubber while they are in the warmer waters.

During this time the whales mate and conceive their young. Well-fed whales, like other animals, make better mates and parents. Scientists noticed that during World

War II blue whales gave birth to more young than they had in previous years. Because so many blue whales had been killed before the war, the ones that were left did not have to share the supply of krill with thousands of other whales. They had all the food they could eat, without being disturbed by whalers.

Whales, like many other animals in the wild, are choosy about their mates. They do not select the first member of the opposite sex that comes along. They may swim together or even touch each other, to see if there is a response. If nothing happens—if the "chemistry" isn't right—the two whales go their own way.

When whales find the right mates they are very loving animals. They enjoy touching each other. They rub their giant bodies against each other and reach out to stroke their mates with their sensitive flippers. They spend many hours in courtship. Humpbacks, in particular, show a lot of affection toward their mates. With their very long flippers, which sometimes grow to fourteen feet, they embrace each other. They splash and roll together in the warm sea.

A whale's body is streamlined so it can move easily through the water. Only its flippers and fins, which it needs for swimming and balance, stick out on its smooth body. Even as its ears and nose are tucked away in its skin, so its sexual parts are tucked away too, and only appear when the animal is mating or suckling its young.

70

The Birth of a Whale

Scientists know very little about the mating of the great whales. Only a few human beings have seen the act. Both whales dive, swim toward each other underwater, and come together with a great burst of speed. Belly to belly, they clasp each other and rise so that their bodies are partly out of water—straight up and down. Then they separate, falling back into the water with a mighty splash that can be heard a long distance across the water.

Although whales are the largest animals on earth, their lives begin on the tiniest scale. A whale's spermatozoa —the seeds of life—are no larger than a man's. The calf begins life as just a tiny speck on the inner wall of its mother's ovary. But from then on it grows rapidly. It must be ready for birth within a year when its mother comes once more to the warm seas.

While her calf is growing, the mother whale swims slowly back toward her usual feeding grounds. She is still taking nourishment from the rich fat and oil stored in her blubber. Some whales, particularly those that live their lives in the Northern Hemisphere, will continue to eat occasionally even when away from their feeding grounds. Since blue whales, living south of the equator, seldom eat during this time, they begin to get hungry on the way to the Antarctic. If they happen to find krill or other suitable food on the way, they will eat it.

Back in the feeding grounds, a whale that is carrying a calf eats in bulging mouthfuls. She never seems to get enough. If somehow she escapes the deadly harpoons, she will be fat and healthy when she returns to warmer waters the next year.

Meanwhile, the calf inside its mother has grown rapidly to be ready to enter the world at the proper moment. At birth a blue whale calf is twenty-five feet long and weighs two tons. A fin whale is about twenty feet long, and most other baleen calves are about fifteen feet.

But as yet the calf has little blubber to protect it. It must be born in warmer seas because it could not stand the cold waters of the polar region. And it must be born soon after the mother returns to the warmer waters. Then it will have a chance to grow a thick coat of blubber before it is time to swim to the feeding grounds.

Most of what we know about the birth of whales comes from scientists who have watched the event take place among the smaller, toothed whales—such as dolphins— in captivity. Whales are generally born tail first. Otherwise, if the head emerged first, the calf might drown before the birth was completed. Muscles within the mother's body finally push the little whale into the world. Since baleen whales do not have teeth, the mother snaps the umbilical cord with a sudden twist of her powerful body.

The moment of birth is a dangerous one for the calf. It has been born underwater where there is no air to breathe. It gasps for air in its strange new world. The mother must work quickly, swimming under the calf and boosting it toward the surface. The little whale, which knows how to swim at birth, has to learn how to breathe properly. If it does not, it will die.

Nudged by its mother's body and guided by her flippers, the little whale breaks the surface of the water and emerges into the fresh air. If the weather is stormy, big waves may pound the young mammal, rolling it over and causing it to suck in more water than air. The mother stays next to the calf to steady it as it takes its first breath. Soon it breathes easily, and is able to dive comfortably with its mother.

The mother keeps her calf close to her—often the calf swims just below its mother's flippers. Sharks, which would not attack an adult whale, might be tempted to snatch a calf that has wandered from its mother. Even when she sleeps, the calf drifts just under her protecting body.

The calf at birth is amazingly well developed. It is a good swimmer and it sees and hears clearly. Like all healthy babies, it has a good appetite. Only a few minutes after it is born and has taken its first breaths, the calf begins to feel hunger.

The mother is aware of her calf's needs. She slows down, barely moving underwater. The calf swims in beneath her tail and moves along her underside. Turning

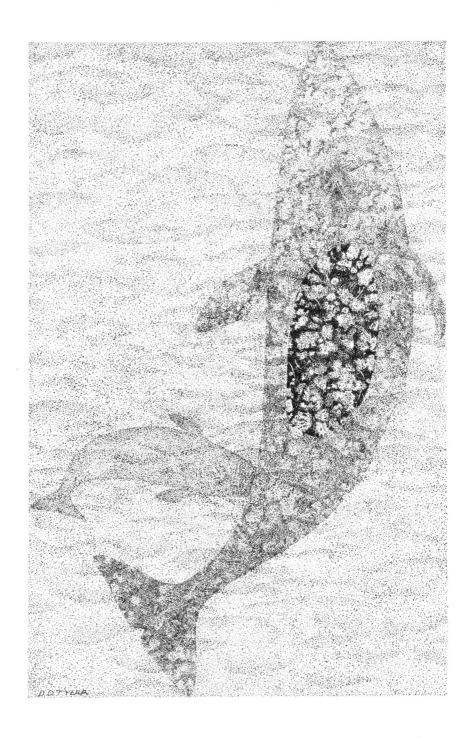

D.D.TYLER

slightly on her side, the mother pushes out a large nipple from a slit in her skin. The calf, which does not have sucking lips as most mammals do, opens its mouth and wraps its tongue around the nipple. It pushes the nipple against the roof of its mouth. Then the mother squirts a stream of creamy white milk into the calf's mouth.

A whale's milk, full of fat, protein, and vitamins, is ten times richer than cow's milk. The young whale may drink as much as fifty gallons a day. A curious scientist who tasted whale's milk says it has a mild, fishy smell and reminds him of a mixture of fish, liver, oil, and milk of magnesia. No wonder it is rich.

One of the few great whales we know much about is the California gray whale. It is the only one of the baleen whales that whalers and scientists have regularly studied for a long time. Its special way of life makes watching it much easier than is the case with the other baleen whales that feed, mate, and give birth in remote parts of the sea.

Scientists call the gray whale the most "primitive" of all the great whales. This means its way of life is closer to the way its ancestors lived than that of other whales. Its long, cigar-shaped body has more hair than whales

---

An aerial view of a gray whale nursing its calf. The dark oval on the mother's back is the part exposed above water.

usually have—about 60 hairs on top of its small head and 120 on the lower jaw. Gray whales don't roam the wide oceans as much as other whales do, either. They feed on small fish and other creatures that are generally found close to shore. They migrate along the coast and, most important for both old-time whalers and the modern scientists, they mate and give birth in shallow, protected water.

There are two populations of gray whales—the California gray whale in North American waters and the Korean herd in Asian waters, which the Japanese have practically wiped out. California gray whales have the longest migration route of any mammals in the world. They spend the summer feeding in the Arctic Ocean and the Bering Sea off Alaska.

When the ice begins to close in, the gray whales migrate south. It takes them about three months to swim from their feeding grounds in the north to their breeding grounds on the coast of Mexico—a distance of between four thousand and six thousand miles.

The gray whale's migration route takes them past the California coast. Thousands of people who love to watch whales look forward to the migration each year. Cub scouts can even earn a merit badge for whale watching! The best place to see the migration on the coast is from the Cabrillo National Monument at Point Loma. Many other people cruise offshore in small boats to watch the whales.

The Birth of a Whale

The whales begin to go past California in December on their way south. Sometimes they put on a spectacular show for the whale watchers. Courting whales pass Point Loma in groups, playing, splashing, and rolling over in the waves. Some of the whales "breach"—hurling their bodies out of the water, twisting in midair, and coming down on their sides or backs in a thunderous splash. Gray whales often "spy hop"—they thrust their heads high out of the water to look around and see where they are.

The goal of the gray whale's migration is the lagoons of Baja California in Mexico. A lagoon is a smaller body of water partly cut off from the sea by rocks or sandbars. While the water is often choppy in these lagoons, it is warm, shallow, and salty. Scientists believe that one of the reasons gray whales give birth in lagoons is because it is easier to float there. Young whales, which do not have a lot of blubber to help them keep afloat, swim with less effort in very salty water.

The most famous of these watery nurseries is Scammon's Lagoon, 350 miles south of San Diego. This lagoon, which is 30 miles long and about 5 miles wide, is bordered by the high white dunes of a desert. The rocks and crashing waves at its entrance would keep out most kinds of large whales. But gray whales make their way easily through shallow water and over the rocks.

Whalers, and not scientists, were the first people to watch whales closely in the lagoon. Captain Charles

Scammon of San Francisco discovered the breeding colony there in 1857. He sailed into the lagoon and found whales all around his ship. It was easy to harpoon them. But these whales, protecting calves that had just been born, fought back fiercely. They rammed the small boats, smashing them to splinters and injuring some of the men. Only when Captain Scammon began to use lances tipped with small bombs was he able to kill the whales and return to San Francisco with a full load.

After that, whalers came regularly to kill the whales in the lagoon. Like other whales, gray whales will not leave their calves—they will stay to defend them even if it means their own death. The whalers knew this and often harpooned or shot the calves. When the mothers rushed in to protect their young, the whalers killed them easily.

Captain Scammon described the lagoon that was named after him:

"The scene of slaughter was exceedingly picturesque and unusually exciting, especially on a calm morning when the whales, as they send forth their towering spouts, frequently tinted with blood, would appear greatly distorted. The boats would be seen gliding over the water, with the colossal form of the whale appearing for an instant like a specter while the report of the bomb-guns would sound like the sudden discharge of musketry. But one cannot fully realize, unless he be an eyewitness, the intense excitement of the reckless pursuit. Numbers of boats will be fast to whales at the same time, and the stricken animals in their efforts to escape can be seen darting in every direction through the water, or breaching headlong clear of the surface, coming down with a splash that sends columns of foam in every direction. The men in the boats shout and yell. It is one continually changing watery battle scene."

The California gray whales nearly became extinct. Some years ago they were given protection in the lagoons, and Mexico made Scammon's Lagoon a national park. Now scientists go there to study the mating of these whales and the birth of their young. The San Diego Natural History Museum has chartered a large boat during the breeding season to take whale watchers there.

The scene in the lagoon today is much different from what it was in Captain Scammon's time. Some of the whales come there to mate. They stroke and clasp each other in the shallow lagoon. In mating, the female rolls on her back, her flippers spread wide, and is embraced by the male.

Other females come to the lagoon to give birth in the warm, salty water. When the wind blows hard, the shallow water grows choppy and the waves crash over the calves' blowholes, making it hard for them to breathe.

But on calm days the whales seem to enjoy themselves in the lagoon. Some roll in the gentle breakers at the lagoon's entrance. Others doze in the sun, looking like enormous floating logs with only a long stretch of back visible to the whale watchers. Their tails hang downward to warn them if they drift into very shallow water. Every five minutes or so the sleeping whale lifts its head to breathe.

The whales remain in the lagoon for only about two months. It is a strenuous time for the females. Their thick coat of blubber holds nourishment for themselves and for their calves. As the calves grow, drinking the rich milk, their mothers lose weight.

Soon the gray whales are at sea again, swimming thousands of miles back up the coast. The nursing calves grow their own coat of blubber that will protect them against the icy waters of the northern ocean. The females will arrive there just in time to begin feeding and fatten up for another year.

8
THE BREATH
OF LIFE

Although whales are the largest animals that have ever lived, they live so far at sea and travel such great distances that they are very hard to study. There are still a lot of questions about how whales live, but we have been too busy killing them to learn about them. Fortunately, scientists are now at work studying them.

What is a whale's spout? This question is not easily answered. Perhaps it can only be answered in several different ways, depending on the kind of whale we are talking about, where it lives, and what it is doing.

Each of the great whales sends up a spout in a different shape. Whalers and whale watchers can often identify the species at some distance just by watching the shape and size of its spout. The blue whale sends up a tall, slender column of spray. The gray whale's spout is low and bushy. The right whale's is V-shaped, almost in the form of a heart. The sperm whale, like the other toothed whales, has only a single blowhole. It is tipped forward and slightly to the left of the head, and the spout is blown forward at an angle.

We already know that the spout is visible when a whale comes to the surface to clear its lungs of stale air. The mammal spouts with a loud *whoooosh* that can be heard a long distance away. Sometimes the spout smells "fishy."

Many scientists say that the spout is caused by the whale's warm, moist breath striking the cooler air outside. We seem to spout too on cold days when we blow out little puffs of "smoke." Other scientists say the spout is made up mostly of tiny drops of oil that a whale gathers in its lungs from its bloodstream while it is underwater.

The gray whale's habit of spending time in shallow lagoons recently gave scientists a chance to study them more closely. Their spout in the warm Mexican water is made up mostly of seawater. Photographs taken by the scientists show that the whale often begins to blow before its blowholes come to the surface. So the whale gets water in its blowholes and shoots it out in a bushy spout as it breaks the surface. When a gray whale is resting at the surface, its blowholes are not completely underwater. When it breathes at those times, it shows no spout at all or only a very tiny one.

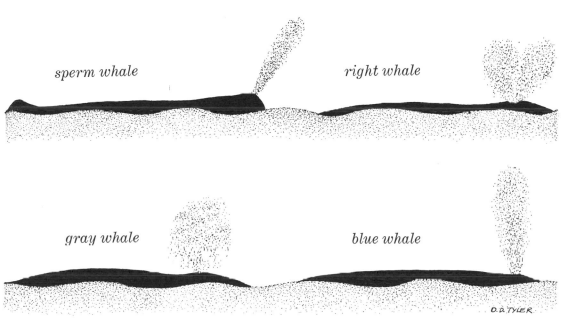

sperm whale

right whale

gray whale

blue whale

D.D.TYLER

Identifying whales by their spouts.

The studies of gray whales in the Mexican lagoons are typical of the new way in which man is looking at these animals. In Robert Cushman Murphy's day, scientists were able to study only dead whales or go along on whaling ships as part of the crew. But modern technology, which was used to kill whales more easily, also helped scientists to find out more about the way whales live. They studied the gray whale's spout with the help of high-speed cameras and sensitive instruments that they attached to the blowholes. The studies helped to show what marvelous creatures whales really are.

Whale Watch

A whale's body is a complicated organism. This mammal, which returned to the sea from land millions of years ago, has developed other ways to deal with life in the oceans. A whale has been called "a great thermos bottle." Its blubber is made up of oil drops held together by strong fibers. When a whale goes without eating for a long time, it can draw nourishment from this rich store of fat. The fibers that make up the blubber are lighter than water. That is why a thick layer of blubber helps a whale to float.

Blubber makes a perfect overcoat. In fact, it sometimes keeps a whale too warm for its own good. A whale, living underwater, does not sweat. But when it is especially active, or it is swimming in warm water, it may grow very warm in its thick coat. To get rid of the extra heat, its blood vessels run close to its body's surface. Some of the heat escapes this way, and some through the flukes and flippers—which are not covered by blubber.

As we have seen, whales are well equipped to capture air at the surface, and to stay warm in all kinds of weather. But the greatest change their bodies made when they gave up their life on land has fitted them to live deep in the sea for many minutes at a time.

When a whale dives, it leaves behind the element that keeps it alive—fresh air. Through its open blowholes it sucks in enormous lungfuls of air. Then it closes the blowholes, lowers its head, and, with a strong kick of its flukes, lowers itself into the sea. When we dive, we keep our mouths shut so that water doesn't flow back into our nasal passages and get into our lungs. But a whale's mouth is not connected to its nasal passages or blowholes. It can swim along with its great mouth wide open, taking in tons of water and krill. Because its blowholes are tightly closed, no water can seep into its lungs.

A baleen whale generally feeds on krill and other animals near the surface. Even so, if it found a dense mass of food, it would not be convenient for the whale to come up every two or three minutes to breathe. The sperm whale, which hunts squid deep in the sea, must stay down for long periods of time.

No other mammals can remain underwater so long. To do so, whales are able to hold their breath while slowing down their body functions. Scientists studied small whales, such as dolphins, in captivity and learned that their heartbeat slows from one hundred a minute to less than fifty underwater.

A whale need not use much energy to swim underwater. Its body is so streamlined and its muscles so powerful that it slides through the water with ease. Blue whales cruise along at about fifteen nautical miles an hour, but they have been watched swimming at nearly twenty-five nautical miles an hour when frightened. Slower whales, such as the humpbacks, may move at about five nautical miles an hour.

Adult whales live primarily underwater. They have

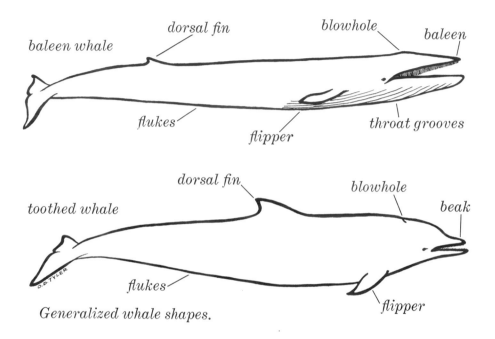

baleen whale · dorsal fin · blowhole · baleen · flukes · flipper · throat grooves

toothed whale · dorsal fin · blowhole · beak · flukes · flipper

Generalized whale shapes.

few enemies there. Sperm whales are often scarred by their battles with the giant squid that they hunt in the depths of the sea. But no matter how fiercely the squid battle for their lives, they usually end up in a sperm whale's stomach.

Just as the most dangerous creatures we are likely to meet in a jungle are mosquitoes and other small biting insects, so the great whales are usually bothered in the sea only by very small animals. Among the peskiest for whales are tiny, crablike parasites called whale lice. They sink their claws into the skin of a whale and suck its blood. Other tiny animals called copepods burrow into the skin and sometimes cause minor infections. They leave little holes in the skin when they die and fall off.

Whale watchers notice that some whales are covered with large clusters of white bumps. These bumps are barnacles—small shellfish that attach themselves in colonies to an object—and are harmless. They attach themselves to any large object in the ocean—rocks, docks, the shells of lobsters, the hulls of ships, and the skin of whales. They are just looking for a place to live and strain their food from the surrounding water, and are most likely to get a foothold on slow-moving whales such as humpbacks. The barnacles found on one dead humpback weighed half a ton.

Scientists say that parasites are usually found on older whales. How old is an "old whale"? No one knows for sure. It is generally believed that whales never live to a ripe old age as some parrots or turtles do, and that thirty or forty years is the limit. Whales have been tagged by biologists so that they can discover where they go and how long they live. The trouble is that whalers don't let whales live very long in any case.

Not long ago scientists found bonelike plugs in the ears of baleen whales that they believe might give them a clue to the mammal's age. These plugs are built up of cells, layer by layer, and it may be that each layer represents one year of age, just as the growth rings tell us a tree's age. Some of these plugs contain eighty layers, which would make the whale eighty years old. But, like much about these fascinating animals, no one can say for sure.

9
THE SMALL WHALES

A place that many people like to visit in Florida or California is an oceanarium. There, in large outdoor pools, bottlenose dolphins, spinner dolphins, killer whales, and other members of the whale family put on a spectacular show. The animals leap from the water to great heights, spin in the air, play with their trainers, and perform a variety of tricks that demand both agility and intelligence.

But these expensive oceanariums do more than give vacationers a pleasant day under a warm sun. They also give scientists a view into the world of whales that they have never had before. As they watch these small whales in captivity, they uncover secrets that show the whales to be among the most remarkable forms of life.

Before World War II, bottlenose dolphins were sometimes caught by fishermen off the Atlantic Coast. Arthur McBride, who was the director of an oceanarium in Florida, wanted to add some of these mammals to his collection. He set up nets to capture them, but he soon learned that the dolphins turned away from the nets long before they reached them. McBride had been reading about the discovery that bats detect barriers in front of them by echolocation—sending out streams of high-pitched sounds that bounce off objects and return to tell the night-flying bats there is something in their way.

McBride knew that dolphins, like all whales, spend most of their lives underwater where little light filters below the surface. Because the dolphins turned from his nets before they could possibly have seen them, he guessed they had found the nets by echolocation too. He put out nets with larger openings, hoping to confuse them. Sure enough, he began to catch dolphins.

During the war, other scientists added to our information about dolphins and whales. Until then, people always thought of the sea as a very quiet place. Whoever heard of a sea creature that roared? Naval engineers put sensitive instruments down into the sea to listen for enemy submarines. While listening for their engines, they heard an almost unbelievable collection of grunts, wails, sighs, and clicks. They learned that some of those sounds were made by whales.

By this time it was clear that whales are more complicated than mankind had imagined. After the war, workers began to catch dolphins for oceanariums. They caught them in nets, then wrapped them in wet blankets to keep them moist, and transferred them on beds of plastic foam to their new homes. If dolphins are treated gently, they will not struggle and injure themselves, though at first many of them died from shock and other causes during transport.

Dolphins soon became popular attractions at oceanariums. One of the most amazing species turned out to be the killer whales. These animals—dreaded by sailors for centuries because they were supposed to be so fierce—do well in captivity and are very gentle with their human trainers. They have even learned to do tricks like other dolphins. In fact, conservationists worry that too many of these whales are being captured in Puget Sound, Washington, for display in oceanariums.

Scientists made use of the oceanariums, studying some whale species there for the first time. Now scientific organizations are keeping dolphins in tanks and pools of their own. It is not yet possible to keep the great baleen whales in captivity because no one can produce enough krill to feed them. There are many people who hope that these giants will never be penned up by humans. In any case, studies on dolphins and porpoises have told us much about whales in general.

These small, toothed whales are intelligent and easy to

train. Dolphins are like people—some have more talent than others. But most dolphins seem eager to cooperate with their trainers. Biologists believe one reason for this may be that they are naturally cooperative and helpful with each other in the wild. This ability to cooperate helps them to survive. Another reason may be that dolphins seem to get bored easily in captivity. Doing tricks helps to pass the time.

There is a species in the Pacific Ocean called the spinner dolphin. Sailors and fishermen have often noticed hundreds of these animals leaping out of the water together, spinning rapidly through the air and plunging back into the ocean. At a large oceanarium a spinner dolphin was put into a tank with a bottlenose dolphin. The trainer had the spinner dolphin do what it does naturally—leap from the water and spin several times in midair. The bottlenose, which lives in the Atlantic Ocean and had never seen a spinner before, suddenly leaped out of the water and—to everyone's astonishment—began spinning too.

Much more important than the dolphins' ability to perform tricks is the way they use sounds. Scientists had already guessed that the toothed whales feed by echolocation, but no one had yet proved that this is so. Two marine biologists, William Schevill and his wife, Barbara Lawrence, made experiments with a bottlenose dolphin in

Massachusetts. They kept the dolphin in a pond of muddy water. Then they silently put a fish on one side of a net or the other, far enough from the dolphin so it could not possibly see it. The dolphin, sending forth a stream of squeaks and clicks, always swam to the correct side of the net to get the fish.

Other biologists made similar experiments to prove that small whales use echolocation. In Florida they sent dolphins through tricky mazes in murky water and even set up two exits, one open and the other covered by transparent plastic. The dolphins always headed for the open one. In other tests these animals were able to choose a fish they liked to eat from one they didn't like—simply by bouncing sounds off it.

The U.S. Navy used this knowledge to get a pilot whale to bring back dummy torpedoes from the ocean floor. The navy attached a radio to the torpedo, which guided the whale to it. By using a special mouthpiece attached to a sling, the whale recovered the torpedo from a depth of over sixteen hundred feet.

Whales use sounds for getting in touch with each other too. Many kinds of whales sing songs just as birds do. The beluga, or white whale, is often called the "sea canary." Many dolphins sing in clear, beautiful whistles, which they repeat over and over again. Each dolphin's song is different from that of others, even from members of its

Beluga, or white whale.

own species. Another dolphin, hearing the song, knows which individual animal is singing it. The animal is singing, "I am a bottlenose dolphin," and also, "I am Anne," or "I am Billy."

Fishermen sometimes heard whales singing because their voices—like some other sounds from water—can be transmitted through wood. A fisherman could actually hear the whale singing through the bottom of his wooden boat. When he was studying humpback whales near Bermuda, a biologist named Roger Payne heard the whales through the bottom of his little wooden rowboat. Later, he went out in a sailboat, which moves noiselessly, towing two hydrophones on long cables. Hydrophones are microphones that pick up underwater sounds. The cables fed the sounds into a tape recorder on the boat. Because he used two hydrophones, Payne recorded the sounds in stereo.

Everyone who listened to the recordings was amazed. They had never heard anything like a humpback's song before. One of the songs, for example, began like a deep moan coming out of a cave. Yet it had a strange melody to it. Then the song rose to a sound like that of a horn in a symphony orchestra. From there the sound faded away on a very high note like the wail of faraway bagpipes. Roger Payne eventually released the songs on a long-playing record.

Whale Watch

In every respect, whales have shown that they are highly intelligent animals. Their brains are very large—the sperm whale has the largest brain any creature has ever had. They also have a highly developed social system, working together and communicating in a complicated way.

Whales are not easily fooled. John Lilly, a student of whales, once planned a film about a porpoise rescuing a man. He asked a friend to jump into a pool with a trained porpoise named Sissy. The man pretended to be drowning. Sissy swam to him and pushed him to the side of the pool where he was safe.

But Lilly forgot to take the cap off the camera lens. He asked the man to jump in the water and do it again. Once more his friend pretended to be in trouble, but once was enough for Sissy. This time she just swam over to him and whacked him with her flipper.

Now, on both coasts, people are receiving much pleasure and knowledge from the small whales. Unfortunately, in the Pacific Ocean there are men who watch these remarkable animals for a different purpose, and it is leading to their destruction. These are the tuna fishermen, who senselessly kill hundreds of thousands of porpoises every year.

Tuna is eaten more widely in America than any other fish. For many years fishing boats followed the yellowfin tuna in the Pacific, catching large numbers of them with

Spotted dolphins, yellowfin tuna, and frigatebirds.

hooks and lines. Canned tuna fish became a national favorite used in both sandwiches and salads. Fishermen sold all the tuna they could catch, but the big canning companies wanted still more.

During the 1950s the fishermen came up with what they thought was a clever idea. They had noticed that whenever they saw certain kinds of porpoises in the Pacific, there was always a large school of tuna swimming just below them. No one is quite sure why these porpoises swim with tuna. Are they following the tuna, or are the tuna following them? They don't bother each other. Perhaps they both feed on the same kinds of fish.

The tuna fishermen bought long nets called purse seines. When they saw the porpoises swimming along on the surface, they lowered the nets into the water and surrounded them, then they tightened the net and pulled up their catch. In this way they caught the entire school of tuna, with much less work than if they had fished for them with hooks and lines.

The trouble is that in this kind of fishing most of the porpoises are killed. They become entangled in the nets and suffocate or die of shock before they can be released. The fishermen have no use for them, so they just dump their lifeless bodies overboard. The spinner dolphin is the species that is most often killed.

Since 1972 it has been against the law for Americans

to kill any kind of whale. The tuna fishermen say they are not deliberately killing the porpoises. That is not true, of course, because when they fish in that way they know they are going to kill thousands of porpoises. Conservationists say that the U.S. government, which is trying to protect the great whales, should also protect small ones such as porpoises. They sued the government to force it to get the tuna industry to obey the law and change the way they fish.

The tuna fishermen, like the whalers, are being short-sighted. In some years they kill over two hundred thousand porpoises. At that rate, they may wipe out the porpoises that help them find tuna, and so they will destroy their own business at the same time. Fortunately, some of the fishermen are now working with biologists to find ways to save dolphins.

Meanwhile, scientists go on investigating the lives of these small whales. We have just begun to understand some of their secrets. We are still learning about how their society is put together—these social animals help each other in many ways, such as in catching food and even in caring for each other's young. By watching them closely we are also beginning to see that play is as important to them as it is to young children of our own species.

It is by studying whales, rather than killing them, that we will truly enrich our own lives.

10
BOYCOTT!

The great whales, supposedly protected by the International Whaling Commission, were dying out by the end of the 1960s. Five species—the blue, right, bowhead, humpback, and gray whales—were nearly extinct. Now whalers were killing mostly fin, sei, Minke, and sperm whales.

Many people realized there would have to be a new method for saving whales. The old idea that there could be a polite agreement among the nations of the world hadn't worked. In the United States, people were calling upon their government to do something quickly. Congress passed a resolution asking all nations to declare a ten-year moratorium on killing the great whales. The U.S. government listed all the great whales as "endangered species." This meant that whale meat, oil, or any other products from their bodies could not be imported into the United States.

Boycott!

The whaling nations still make a great many products from these animals. Baleen whales are used as meat mainly in Japan; the meat of the toothed whales, such as the sperm whale, has too strong a flavor for most people. But otherwise, whale bodies are ground up for use in many products, including certain detergents and industrial lubricating oils. Sperm whales also produce a gray, waxy substance in their intestines. This is called ambergris and is used in the manufacture of perfumes.

Oil from various whales is thick and fatty and serves as a base for cosmetics and crayons. After being treated, it also goes into the making of varnish, linoleum, printing ink, soap, and gelatin. Oil from fin whales is mixed with vegetable oil to make margarine. The guts and other parts of whales are ground up and canned as pet food or sometimes mixed with wheat bran as cattle feed.

A hundred years ago there was a need for oil and other products made from whales, but many people now believe that it no longer makes sense to kill these rare animals for such purposes. Every product made from whales today can be made from substitute materials.

Until the U.S. government declared the sperm whale an endangered species, this country imported fifty million pounds of its oil every year. When scientists began to look for substitute oils, they found a remarkable plant called the jojoba that grows in the deserts of the U.S. Southwest and Mexico. The seeds of this shrub are

Jojoba plant.

pressed to extract an oil that will replace sperm whale oil. The plant is easily cultivated in dry regions, and twelve pounds of its seeds yield six pounds of oil. This shrub, which hardly anybody ever noticed before, may help to save the sperm whale from extinction.

The knowledge that substitutes can be found for all whale products encouraged people to petition for a moratorium on killing whales, but the International Whaling Commission had no power. When twelve of the fourteen member nations voted to cut down on the number of whales that could be killed in 1973, Japan and Russia objected—so the ruling was not adopted. The Japanese also own a large whaling company in Peru, a country which does not even belong to the commission. That company can go on killing whales without restriction.

It was then that a number of conservation groups in the United States decided to boycott all products made in Japan and Russia. The word boycott has an interesting history. Captain Boycott was an agent for wealthy landowners in Ireland. He treated the local people so badly that finally they refused to have anything to do with him. They "boycotted" him. This is just what American conservation organizations such as the National Audubon Society and the National Wildlife Federation asked their members to do—boycott the goods produced by the countries that went on destroying whales.

Whale Watch

How does a boycott work? First of all, the conservation organizations asked their members not to visit Japan or Russia or buy their products. The idea was that, even if these countries did not care whether the whales survived, they might be alarmed by the thought of losing American dollars. Eighteen conservation organizations, with their five million members, supported the boycott. They also asked their members to write to the governments of Japan and Russia to tell them how they felt about the killing of whales.

Some conservationists bought advertising space in newspapers to tell their side of the story to the public. The ads told how many whales are being killed each year, what marvelous animals they are, and why killing them is senseless. One ad in a large newspaper had this to say about whales:

"We needn't wait for the galaxies to send us intelligent non-human life so that we might begin communications. *Intelligent, non-human life* exists in this planet's oceans, right now, and we are making it into pet food, car wax, machine oil and lipstick."

Conservationists distributed buttons and T-shirts with pictures of whales, and bearing such slogans as Save the Whales and Boycott Japanese Goods. Groups such as the Rare Animal Relief Effort—called RARE—organized demonstrations in front of buildings that belonged to

Boycott!

Japanese and Russian companies. They asked people to sign petitions that protested the killing of whales. When these petitions were filled with signatures, RARE sent them to the Japanese and Russian governments.

Many people stopped buying goods made by those two countries. They stopped buying their cars, motorcycles, cameras, and binoculars. *Audubon*, the magazine of the National Audubon Society, stopped selling ad space for Japanese cameras and binoculars. This meant that the magazine lost the income made from printing the ads, but its editors believe that whales are more important than money.

Children played a part in the campaign too. A conservation group called Project Jonah urged children to write letters to the Japanese government. In 1974 three girls from the United States, Canada, and Sweden took seventy-five thousand of these letters to Tokyo and gave them to the premier of Japan. All of the letters asked the Japanese to stop killing whales.

The boycott had more of an effect than the efforts of the International Whaling Commission in previous years. For example, an executive of a large import company that sells Japanese food products in the United States wrote to the Japanese government and said he had received many letters from buyers who said they would refuse to buy any more of their products unless Japan

Even the much-feared killer whale is now looked upon in a better light.

stopped killing whales. The executive suggested that the Japanese government change its attitude toward whales.

The Japanese government became alarmed about the boycott. It hired a public-relations company in New York to try to convince Americans that there is no harm in killing thousands of whales every year. Eli Gabel, a public-relations man for this company, wrote a letter to *The New York Times*, saying that Japan needed whale meat for its people. He also said that Japan respected the International Whaling Commission's restrictions on the killing of whales.

The editors of the *Times*, which is one of the leading newspapers in the United States, wrote an editorial in reply. It said that Gabel was mistaken, then went on to describe how Japan and Russia have always fought against regulations that would help to save the whales from extinction, and that it was nonsense to say that Japan kills whales simply for food—half of the whales that Japan kills now are sperm whales, which are rarely eaten. The Japanese people do not depend heavily on whale meat for their protein. Whale meat, *The Times* editors wrote, "is less than 2% of their total protein intake, which comes from fish, shellfish and soybeans, as well as meat." The Japanese have so much protein that they export fish to other countries.

Did it help the whales for Americans to boycott Japanese and Russian goods? Did it help to write letters and sign petitions? Did it help to try to get the true story about the killing of whales to the American people?

At recent meetings of the International Whaling Commission, the representatives of Japan and Russia have not been quite so fiercely opposed to the other members' suggestions. They will not agree to a ten-year moratorium on the killing, but they agree to lower the number of fin whales they kill each year. They also agree to let the Whaling Commission study sperm whales to see if they are endangered, and if there are more humane ways to kill whales than with explosive heads on harpoon guns. In 1977 many conservation groups agreed that Japan had changed its whaling industry to a great extent. They halted the boycott against Japanese products.

These are small steps toward the protection of the endangered animals. Many people have fought hard to get even this much done. It takes extensive planning and hard work to have an effect on an issue that involves so many countries all over the world. But people who are concerned about whales believe they are worth fighting for.

One of the people who has fought hard to save the whales is Robert M. White, a U.S. representative on the International Whaling Commission. He wrote a letter to the head of one of the conservation groups:

"I think there has been a marked change in world attitudes regarding the conservation of whales. This change has been brought about by the public education efforts carried out by your organization and several other private citizen groups. The plight of the whale has brought many of us together for the first time and I think helped to demonstrate the effectiveness of concerted action."

11
A NEW ATTITUDE

Jim is a fisherman, and in good weather he is out on the ocean in his boat off the coast of Maine almost every day. On a fine day in August he was near the lighthouse at Mount Desert Rock. As he went past the island he waved to Ben and the other observers who were looking out to sea for whales.

Like other fishermen along the coast, Jim has been asked by the College of the Atlantic to report any whales he sees. The college sends him printed forms to gather information for its study of whales. When Jim sees one, he fills out a form that tells where he saw it, how large it was, what it looked like, how many times it spouted, and in which direction it was headed. He notes the time of day when the whale appeared, the weather, and the condition of the sea. Then he returns the form to the college.

A New Attitude

When Jim was several miles past the lighthouse he saw a commotion in the water. There was another boat ahead of him and alongside it there was something thrashing and rolling, tossing water about as if it were in trouble.

Jim knew at once that it was a big whale, and for a moment he thought the people on the boat had harpooned it. He turned up his engine to full speed and headed for the spot to see what had happened, determined that he would try to protect the whale. The boat sped across the water. A flock of seabirds scattered out of its way. Only when Jim drew close to the whale and the other boat did he relax, and then his face broke into a broad grin. It was a humpback, playing on the surface. The people on the other boat were standing by the rail, watching the scene with astonishment.

Jim drifted up alongside the other boat and turned off the engine. It was pleasant to see such a huge creature enjoying itself. The humpback slapped the water with its long, light-colored flippers. It rolled first on one side and then on the other. It lifted its wide, ragged flukes high in the air and brought them down on the water with a tremendous crash, the water spurting in all directions.

It was some time before Jim realized that the humpback was not alone. On all sides of his boat he saw great dark mounds breaking the water's surface. There would be a long stretch of dripping back and then the blade of a fin as a fin whale began its dive. In another direction he saw the gaping mouth and the long curtain of baleen as a right whale came to the surface. Gulls and other seabirds hovered low over the water, ready to snatch small fish stirred up by the whales.

The whales had come to feed in the rich waters off the Maine coast. The cold blue sea seemed alive with their fins and flukes. Tomorrow the college and its study group, Allied Whale, would receive dozens of reports about this gathering of whales and thus add to humanity's knowledge about these rare and remarkable animals.

Perhaps even more important than the facts and figures in the reports was something much harder to put down on paper. It was the sympathy these creatures of another species now stirred in millions of people around the world. If only we give them the chance, whales may continue to provide us with pleasure and a sense of companionship for all time to come.

A lobster boat surrounded by humpbacks, fin whales, and right whales.

ACKNOWLEDGMENTS

The following books were extremely useful to use in our research:

Carrighar, Sally. *The Twilight Seas: A Blue Whale's Journey*. New York: Weybright and Talley, 1975.

Mowat, Farley. *A Whale for the Killing*. Boston: Little, Brown, 1972.

Murphy, Robert Cushman. *Logbook for Grace*. New York: Macmillan, 1947.

Tryckare, Tre, ed. *The Whale*. New York: Simon & Schuster, 1968.

Walker, Theodore J. *Whale Primer*. San Diego: Cabrillo Historical Association, 1962.

We would like to thank Ben Baxter, Steve Katona, and Jim Salisbury for sharing with us their own experience with whales.

—ADA AND FRANK GRAHAM

INDEX

115